AT MAXWELL STREET

TOM PALAZZOLO'S
AT MAXWELL STREET

CHICAGO'S HISTORIC MARKETPLACE RECALLED
IN WORDS AND PHOTOGRAPHS

Wicker Park Press

Published in 2008 by
Wicker Park Press, Ltd.
P.O. Box 5318
River Forest, Illinois 60305-5318
www.wickerparkpress.com

Library of Congress Cataloging-in-Publication Data on file with the publisher

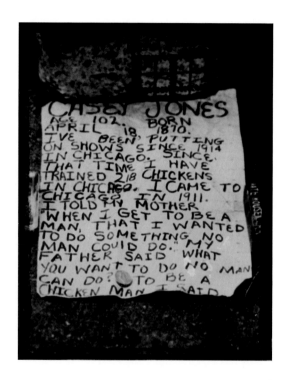

DEDICATED TO THE MEMORY OF CASEY JONES
AND ALL WHO WORKED AT THE MARKET

CASEY JONES: 1870–1974—Mr. Jones was often arrested for not having a street entertainers license. In court he would perform with his chicken for the judge and often win a dismissal. After his death a friend took care of his one remaining chicken.

FISH CRIER

I KNOW a Jew fish crier down on Maxwell Street with a
voice like a north wind blowing over corn stubble
in January.

He dangles herring before prospective customers evincing
a joy identical with that of Pavlowa dancing.

His face is that of a man terribly glad to be selling fish,
terribly glad that God made fish, and customers to
whom he may call his wares, from a pushcart.

—Carl Sandburg

PHOTOGRAPH MARCIA PALAZZOLO

CONTENTS

DVD OF "AT MAXWELL STREET" ON INSIDE BACK COVER

FOREWORD

LORI GROVE

Maxwell Street evolved from a 19th century Old World European street market, and blossomed in 20th century America as Chicago's official open-air market. In true carnivalesque form, street vendors at the Maxwell Street Market developed pitches and props to catch the attention of passers-by or bellowed out syncopated sing-songs. Store merchants hired "pullers" to physically pull shoppers into their stores. The Sunday market was a three-tiered shopping extravaganza composed of the sidewalk storefront shop, the curbside vending shed, and the vending plywood table-tops on wooden horses lining each side of the street. Vehicular traffic was impossible there due to the dense pedestrian population milling, moving, bobbing, and buying on Maxwell Street.

Carl Sandburg wrote his poem the *Fish Crier* about Maxwell Street; Clarence Darrow wrote his short story *Little Louie Epstine* about Maxwell Street; and Bobette Zacharias (a lesser-known author) wrote her mother's memoir entitled *Mama's Maxwell Street*. Throughout almost a full century that the Market occurred on Maxwell Street, photographers continued to photograph it and filmmakers continued to film it. Maxwell Street had a character that inspired its visitors and occupied "a place" much larger than a single residential street. Street life thrived there and its ready-made audience was entertained by Blues and gospel musicians, proselytizers, animated pitchmen hawking their wares, bartering vendors, and the resourceful merchants-in-residence. Maxwell Street served as a platform for humanity where, in the mix of its masses, "the only color that mattered was green." It was Chicago's most enduring, home-grown public space where transient cultures met and mingled, and recognized how to coexist.

Lori Grove, Maxwell Street Foundation, 2008.

MAXWELL STREET

JACK HELBIG

Every Sunday morning the Maxwell Street market seemed to spontaneously appear in open land along Halsted, a few blocks south of Roosevelt. A messy, sprawling open-air flea market where you could find almost anything provided you were willing to poke through piles of junk, check out every stall and table and blanket laid out in no particular order. TVs, radios, clothing, hub caps, spare tires, car paint, old furniture, vinyl records, paperback books, knick-knacks, tchotchkes, just plain junk. And off to one side of the huge urban field, opened up, I suppose, by urban renewal, was often a makeshift blues band wailing away.

The rumor was that some of the items for sale were hot, only recently liberated from the home of some unsuspecting fellow Chicagoan. And some of them probably were. But surely not everything at Maxwell Street was hot.

(At least that is what you told yourself as you bought a five dollar wrench set. Or a graceful little white figurine.)

This was the Maxwell Street I first remember in the early 1970s, when I fled to Chicago from the much more sterile place I grew up in, a few hundred miles away to the southwest. For a sheltered sub-urban white boy used to clean, well lit shopping malls, the messy anarchy of Maxwell Street thrilled me, like the vaguely nasty music that permeated the air.

As a guidebook to Chicago (*Sweet Home Chicago*) put it in the late 1980s: "On Maxwell Street you'll find 43 pairs of your favorite tangerine-colored knee socks for 50 cents a pair or 4 electric typewriters and 6 adding machines for 5 dollars apiece if you take them all now. Of course the knee socks slip down to your ankles and the typewriters are in Hebrew, but how can you pass on such bargains?"

(Full disclosure, I helped write those sentences. The story of the typewriters is true, although in retrospect I think they must have been Yiddish typewriters not Hebrew ones [which would type the other way, right?].)

I never bought anything at Maxwell Street. I went for the people, the heady mix of humanity, the whole jumbled up Chicago jambalaya, Black and White, Latino and Asian, buying and selling and milling around. And I went because Maxwell Street felt, even then, somehow more real than much of Chicago.

For one, Maxwell Street had been around a long time, going back at least to the early 1900s, when Jewish immigrants manned the tables. They were followed by black merchants and later Latinos. In the 1980s more and more Asians were setting up shop there. The place had history—and you could feel it. And hear it in the blues. And smell it in the frying onions that wafted over from the stands selling "hot dog polish porkchop fries."

For another, Maxwell Street was overwhelmingly integrated. Scan the crowds and you saw cross sections of Chicago: prosperous and poor, white and Latino, Black and Asian, all hanging out and doing what we like to do best in America—getting and spending, making a quick buck and losing it even quicker.

These days, if the original Maxwell Street still existed, it would put to shame the parts of Chicago that have been gentrified and Disney-fied almost out of existence—Old Town Land, Lincoln Park. What next? Little Village Land?

I know that Tom Palazzolo, Marcia Palazzolo, and Bernie Beckman used to spend a lot of time at the old Maxwell Street, hanging out and taking pictures. They started in the early 1960s when they were art students in Chicago, studying at the School of the Art Institute of Chicago and the School of Design (now part of the Illinois Institute of Technology).

One of my most vivid memories of Maxwell Street involves Tom Palazzolo and a day my then girlfriend (now wife) Sherry Kent and I met him there for a day of filming. He and his friend Allen Ross (who lived in a huge loft across the street from Maxwell Street) had set down their equipment for just a moment and discovered an expensive 16mm movie camera was missing.

Assuming they had just misplaced it they looked around, retraced their steps, and found nothing. Now at this point in the story many would have just gone to the police, reported the loss, and kicked themselves for not having insurance.

This is not what happened that day.

As often happens, a helpful person arrived, in the guise of a thin young man, no older than thirteen, with a large grin. Tom, always hip to these things, asked him if he could help them find their camera, and offered a small fee for the service.

The young man agreed to help. They might, he told them, find what they were looking for across the street at Maxwell Street.

Tom and Allen started combing the flea market, checking out the wares on display on every table and blanket. They found a lens cap here, set between a cigarette lighter and an ashtray, a lens there, next to an old lamp. The film magazine was at a table way across the lot.

Bit by bit, five dollars here, twenty dollars there, they were able to put the camera back together—all except one large section, which they found (after paying a ransom) hidden inside the basement door of Ross's own building.

I can't remember if Tom and Allen filmed that day. Or if they spent it reassembling their camera.

I do know that Tom and Marcia and Bernie spent plenty of other days documenting the wild wonderful jumbled up relentlessly funky and real world that was old Maxwell Street. As the following pages will attest.

MAXWELL STREET AS I REMEMBER IT

LIONEL BOTTARI

My dad was an immigrant from Italy, and although he had a trade—he was a butcher—he came to Chicago to try to become as great a success financially as his foreign fourth-grade education would allow. He sought any opportunity open to him, and the best one came in the form of the Maxwell Street flea market.

Maxwell Street provided all the pieces to the puzzle of the American dream for him. It gave him access to expertise and connections to services he otherwise wouldn't have had. It also offered him a market where he could resell for a profit whatever he could find or buy at a low price, and he could also sell whatever he produced with his own efforts, using the tools and "junk" he bought on Sundays.

It made it possible for him to buy a home in Chicago's Pilsen neighborhood, with a large basement that he used as a shop during the Second World War. There he cut down adult bicycles with frames he bought on Maxwell Street, and welded them back into children's bicycles with the torches he acquired there, too. No children's bikes were available in those years, and the money made it possible to raise a family. I was born in October of 1942.

As soon as I was big enough, at the age of five or six, I was already helping my father by spotting saleable castoffs and junk that he could pick up with his truck after work. Saturday night was devoted to loading, with all the junk tied on with a web of ropes and cords that discouraged thievery. I had to get up and dress myself at five in the morning on Sunday to be ready to go to Maxwell Street.

In those days the market was west of Halsted Street, before the expressway was built, and it seemed endless. In the bitter winters, my dad would leave me alone to "watch the store" while he prowled for bargains in bicycle junk and tools; I still have his wheel truing stand, dated 1896, and his adjustable spoke wrench, dated 1898. Everything he needed was there, and I was to repeat his experience 20 years later when I founded the Turin Bike Shop, also from tools and parts gleaned on Maxwell Street.

But in those days, I froze, agonizing over what price to charge for the junk we had spread out on the tarpaulin in front of me. Our spot was a good one for commerce but bad in cold weather, as it was in front of a center pillar supporting the railroad viaduct where the wind whistled through constantly.

My father had some strange theories about other races, but all that was forgotten in the camaraderie around the burning garbage cans; his favored companions were the black harmonica players he could jam with at one stand, and one guy in particular who called himself Preacher. Later on, when Pa bought a piece of land in Indiana, all the wintertime road kill of opossums and raccoons we harvested along the road were kept frozen until they could gratefully be accepted by Preacher and his crew.

The best guy in my book was Jake Yanowicz, a Jewish immigrant from Poland, another "junk" dealer like my father. Jake was the sweetest, most generous guy on the whole street. One time in the late 1950s, when I was already a young teenager and shopping on the street on my own, I saw a terrific bargain that I didn't have the money to buy. I stopped to say hello to Jake, and mentioned the fact. To my surprise, he immediately pulled out his roll of dollar bills and offered me a loan. I bought the item, an 1863 Remington Zoave rifle from the Civil War for seventeen dollars. It was the first loan I ever received in my life, and I still appreciate it. I moved heaven and earth in the following weeks to get the money to pay Jake back, and he didn't even ask for any interest. In my heart I thank him still.

Many years later I learned from one of the sock sellers on Maxwell and Halsted Streets that Jake had passed away suddenly, while loading a toilet into his station wagon. He was around eighty years old by then, having outlived my father by a decade or more, and it was probably the way he would have wanted to go, doing what he enjoyed. To me, he was the Prince of Maxwell Street.

Jake typified a lot of the old Maxwell Street Ashkenazim; he was a tough guy, who could defend himself very well, but who had a heart of gold. When you dealt with those old Jewish people on Maxwell Street, their top priority wasn't just to make the immediate sale, but

to establish a relationship with you, hopefully one that would last a lifetime. They wanted you as their client, they wanted you as a customer permanently, a friend on a first name basis to who they could offer a good deal—and from whom they might expect a little extra for something really special. "To you, wholesale price," or, "Take it for ten cents, go ahead, but come back and buy something next week."

In my father's efforts to raise capital for his projects (paying off the house, buying a truck, buying a car) he tried to save money any way he could, and Maxwell Street served as a place where the cheapest children's clothes, new and most often used, could be found. The best example of this that I can think of were called "bundled" socks: six pairs of socks, held together with a band of paper, that sold for the price two pair might ordinarily go for.

But when we took the bundle apart, we found that the outer two socks were perfect, the inner two less so, and the center of the bundle were the rags that resulted when the machines got jammed up, or ran into the end of the material, or got mismatched. These fragments had been sewn back together into some semblance of their original form, then hidden in the middle of the bundle. But we had to wear them anyway.

"Brogans" described a pair of heavy work shoes, made child size, which had steel plates screwed into the heel and toe so that they would last forever. My father decided to invest in these shoes because as we outgrew them they could be passed down the line of the brothers until they could make a cripple out of the youngest. Many years later, socializing with some black guys during the jazz festival, I discovered we had Maxwell Street, bundled socks and brogans as a common thread in our childhood reminiscences.

When I graduated from grammar school, my father took me "down Maxwell Street" to buy me a suit. We let the "pullers," Jew-

A SUDDEN CHILL ON MAXWELL STREET

LINDA PLATT

My family, in the 1950s, lived in the poorest neighborhood in Chicago: the Back of the Yards. Actually, the black neighborhoods were probably poorer, but they weren't counted back then. Our neighborhood was like a very small town. Everyone came from the same village in Southern Poland, used the same spices in their sausage, and knew details about everyone else's lineage; until my father went overseas during World War II. He married a young orphan from the Western border of Poland and brought her home to the grimy, stinking Stockyards. My mother's accent sounded German, and she "put on airs," as the neighbors said. She was hypersensitive, nervous, and quick to anger, and someone I kept my distance from. As a result, I was always shopping for mothers among the ladies I passed on the street.

One of my best opportunities came when I was five years old. My mother arranged for her sister Hilda and her husband to emigrate to the U.S. from Germany. I remember going to the magnificent Dearborn Street train station to meet them, the steam rising as the train slowed in, and the long parade of strangers. Finally there she was: a stiffly smiling woman in a beige suit with pretty shiny buttons and a rhinestoned hat, and her homely husband, Uncle John. They brought me a bride doll from Germany, which my mother wouldn't allow me to play with because it was too delicate. Aunt Hilda reminded me of a lady I had seen on T.V.—Zsa Zsa Gabor—who I didn't think would make a very good mother. But Aunt Hilda had the extra added attraction of gold teeth that flashed like jewelry. Uncle John quickly scooped me up off the ground and tickled me ferociously until I managed to push his hand away.

"Zat's vat you get forr not zmilink," he said, cuddling me as if I were a baby. He carried me, the bride doll, and two big suitcases all the way to our car, where he sat me on his lap and sat the doll on Aunt Hilda's lap. As my father drove to our house, I noticed something even more amazing than their gold teeth. Uncle John was missing the first finger on his right hand! When he noticed me staring at it, he started tickling me again.

My new relatives temporarily took over my bedroom and I was moved to the couch. "Nosink iz forever," said Uncle John. Aunt Hilda sniffed at the neighborhood and wrinkled her nose. "Oh mine Gott! Zis is fallink apart like Europe!" she said.

"All you people think the streets are paved with gold in America," said my father. I didn't know what they were talking about, but it was the first time I felt not really poor, because we had enough to eat and a place to live—but I felt like my neighborhood was a place that other people didn't like.

My father got the idea to play tour guide, and took them on short trips around the city. He started with Douglas Park, which had a beautiful pond with fountains and real swans and water lilies, surrounded by tall white columns. They liked that. My father took a picture of everyone smiling to prove it. When my aunt and uncle found an apartment further down our block and needed pots and pans and towels and furniture, my father thought of taking them to Maxwell Street. They didn't have jobs yet and that's where the best bargains were. My mother didn't like the idea. "That's where poor people go," she said.

I have heard, since then, some people refer to it as "Jew Town." But my father had some Jewish friends from the Army - maybe that's why we didn't use that term. Or maybe it was because of something I learned later: that he had helped liberate one of the concentration camps and saw first hand the potential result of isolating people. "Maxwell Street is just like the street markets in You-rrrope," my father said, imitating Aunt Hilda's pronunciation. She didn't notice that he was teasing her.

When we got out of the car, she held my hand and walked along slowly with me. My mother always seemed to be rushing along, but Aunt Hilda took her time.

It was a lively place, with long rows of old stores on both sides of the cobblestone street, tables set up on the sidewalks, racks hung with clothing, and piles of linens. I was drawn to a sharp-eyed old woman in a babushka, who had bolts of flowery fabric propped up against a building, with big jars of buttons on the sidewalk. I wanted to go up to her and inspect the fabrics, but was gently pulled along towards other things. All the sellers called out to the passersby, hungry for attention. So different from today's malls, where the salespeople look bored to death. Even the people selling things like rusty car parts or used shoes, made their merchandise seem like it was valuable, you were really getting a good deal and shouldn't try to ignore them. Their prices got lower and their voices called out louder as you walked away.

And, of course, there was the smell that made everyone hungry. It was called "Maxwell Street Polish" sausage, but it was nothing like our sausage. My aunt and uncle had to get some, their first taste of American food.

As we walked along, a strange thing began to happen. It seemed as if some of the sellers knew my aunt and uncle. An old guy called out "Hildegarde!" and said something in a language I didn't understand. Aunt Hilda acted like she didn't know him. The sellers started calling out to one another, some of them pointing at their teeth. Then a man selling army surplus called "Johannes!" and some strange last name that I didn't know. My aunt and uncle froze in their tracks. Soon it seemed that all the sellers were shouting at them and shaking their fists. "What's going on?" asked my father.

"I don't know," said Aunt Hilda. "Let's go home. I don't like it here."

Uncle John scooped me up and turned to leave.

"But you didn't even buy anything!" my father protested.

"It's all garbage. Schmata," said Aunt Hilda. They hurried back towards the car.

My father had a long talk with my mother that evening. They argued right in front of my aunt and uncle. My parents spoke Polish, but every so often Aunt Hilda would say something to my mother in some other language. Something terrible and important was happening, but it wasn't for me to know. Without explanation, my new relatives moved out the next morning. They stayed in a hotel, and within a very short time they would move to Florida. They moved around a lot after that too.

It took many years before I understood what happened that day. I asked my father first. "Your mother lied to me," he said. "Hilda and John were Nazis. That's why those people knew them."

"What are Nazis?" I asked.

"Those are the bad guys I was fighting against in the war."

My aunt and uncle were bad? But my uncle was so nice to me, and my aunt was—well . . . pretty.

I waited until my mother was in a good mood to ask her about it. She said, "My sister had to work for the Germans. We were very poor and that was the only job she could get. She was nineteen and they took her to work in a camp. My brothers had to go into the German army too."

"What did Aunt Hilda do in the camp?" I asked, picturing a kind of summer camp in the woods.

"She worked for a dentist."

"What about Uncle John?" I asked.

"Well, he was in the German army. That's how they met."

"Do you mean the Nazi army?"

"Yes. We all had to do what the Nazis told us to do. We were poor."

"I wouldn't have sided with the bad guys," I said.

"We didn't know they were bad," said my mother.

I started reading books on the Holocaust when I was about twelve. Years later, I figured out the explanation for that sudden chill on Maxwell Street. The Nazis, among all the other indignities, had their

dentists remove the gold fillings from their victims' teeth before they killed them. The gold was melted down and put into the treasury.

A few years ago, Aunt Hilda learned that she was dying. She sent everyone little souvenirs to remember her by. I got her wooden sewing box, made in Germany: full of buttons, delicate scissors, and broken jewelry. I found the shiny buttons from that beige suit she wore the first time I saw her. And two other odd buttons, diamond shaped, with two lightning bolts on each. Not really buttons I guess—maybe they were cuff links. Holding them in my hand, turning them around, I realized that what at first looked like abstract shapes were the letters S.S. That's what my uncle did during the war.

PHOTOGRAPH TOM PALAZZOLO

13

BERNARD BECKMAN

Bernard Beckman attended the School of the Art Institute of Chicago in the early 1960s. Although primarily a painter; Beckman often visited the Maxwell Street market to photograph with Tom and Marcia Palazzolo. His photographs reflect a life-long interest in blues and gospel music, as well as a painter's eye for composition, sometimes with a touch of humor. These photos were taken about 1965, around the time Beckman won the Potter Palmer Prize in painting at the annual Chicago and Vicinity Show at the Art Institute of Chicago.

Beckman has since moved to Maine where he continues to paint, teach and exhibit his work. Further information about Beckman's work can be found on his web site www.berniebeckman.com.

Bernie remembers buying his first 35mm camera in 1963. He paid 25 dollars for a used Werra made in East Germany. It had a twin lens reflex with an unusual film winding mechanism. You advanced the film and cranked the shutter via the lens neck. He still has the camera.

Blind Arvella Gray

Gospel Group

Sister Carrie Robinson and Gospel Group

Jim Brewer

PHOTOGRAPH TOM PALAZZOLO

MARCIA PALAZZOLO

Maxwell Street was a place of mystery and intrigue for me growing up. The children in our family were never allowed to go along with my father and uncles when they made their trips early on Sunday mornings. While we kids were in Sunday school they were finding things like replacement hubcaps, spare parts for our old swing set, and a screen door for the back entryway that never quite fit after alterations.

The reason the market at Maxwell Street was on Sunday was due to its origins as a Jewish neighborhood. Saturday is the Sabbath for Jews and so logically the market and shopping day was Sunday, the beginning of the week and still part of the weekend. I finally made it to the famous corner of Halsted and Maxwell as a photography student attending the nearby Illinois Institute of Technology. While I found the corner visually interesting on a weekday, Sundays were the most exciting for me.

In the mid 1960s I would go on photographic jaunts to Maxwell Street with Tom Palazzolo. We were dating at the time, and we would find we had many of the same kinds of pictures, and we found out that we were attracted to the same things, and to each other.

We married a few years later, and would continue to visit the market over the years, never coming home empty-handed. The bargains were abounding. The banter and negotiating was so much fun we often bought things we really didn't need, although occasionally we found something useful.

I still use a large pot I bought there in 1966. Maxwell Street was especially interesting to Tom who had already begun exploring the unique aspects of the city on film. We continued to be attracted to the energy and variety of the week-to-week offerings of the market.

What follows is a glimpse of what I photographed there.

1335
OLD DUTCH ROOT BEER
OLD DUTCH ROOT BEER
OLD DUTCH ROOT BEER

Dr. Johnson with Fez and full regalia

String Game

SALE AWAY

JOHN PLATT

Hey gimme a
You wanna?—Hey
Gimme a—Heymister!
Heymister—Miss—
Missus—Hey!
               Kid, getawayfromthere!

Youwannit?   Ornot?

Heymister!
REDHOTICECOLDBRANDNEWLIKENEWGETITRIGHTHERE

   Whitecane
           Black Blues
                 Full Gospel
                         OhhhJesusgonnatakeme
                                 Spoh-dee-oh

Heymister We Habla Mowimy Heymister
Your Fortune Here Poorboy—Pork Chop
Sandwich—GOINGGOINGGOINGGOING

OUT OF BUSINESS LOST OUR LEASE NO PARKING

               Maddog Heymstrrr
               Four Roses Heymm . . . ann, cann you. . . .

               Heymister please . . .

SALESALESALESALESALESALESALESALESALESALESALE . . .

TOM PALAZZOLO

My interest in Maxwell Street dates back to the early 1960s. As a photography student at the School of the Art Institute of Chicago, I took a class taught by Ken Josephson. In that class I was required to turn in proof sheets and prints every week. Every week!

My practice was (and still is) to put things off until the last minute. I needed a location with loads of subject matter—Maxwell Street was a natural. I could go there on a Sunday morning; shoot quickly, go home, develop and print the pictures, and have them ready for Monday's class. I always had more shots than any of the other students, but they were never as carefully printed. I hoped that Mr. Josephson would ignore quality and grade on volume. He didn't.

After a few photo trips to the market, I started to like what I was getting and enjoyed the experience. It was like stepping back in time, reminding me of photographers from the past, like Lewis Hine and Jacob Riis. I also liked the WPA photographs from the 1930s: socially conscious work that sidestepped any reference to fine art but was more than an objective record. Their humanism inspired me.

Early on I began taking along my girlfriend, Marcia, a photography student at IIT. More disciplined than me, she always checked her light meter before shooting a picture. In addition she had a keener eye for knick-knacks.

We would grab lunch at *Jimmie's Original—Best Fried Fries In Town, Polish Sausage, Hamburgers, Pork Chops and Vienna Hot Dogs* (corner of Halsted and Maxwell Streets). At first we went Dutch on the polish, but when the relationship got serious I paid for hers.

The market was like a huge outdoor theater, with vendors competing for center stage—shouting, singing, bargaining, imploring, threatening, and grabbing you by the sleeve. Impulse buying got hold of us as we sometimes competed for ownership of "treasures," bidding against each other on the price of a carnival souvenir (a chalk ware dog, or Betty Boop). The usual convention at the market was to bid down—not up. At home that afternoon we gloated over our acquisitions. It usually took us a month or so to misplace them.

Adding to the confusion we would often switch cameras while shooting at Maxwell Street, consequently we are not always sure who shot what, let alone when. We married expecting that we would sort things out eventually.

The photographs that follow are more or less in chronological order starting in 1962, and ending in 2000 when the market was all but gone, pushed out by politicians, developers, and UIC, erasing yet another chunk of the city's soul.

Tom photographing at the market with my camera

Above and facing page: Dr. Johnson

Jim's Polish

Community Garden

PHOTOGRAPH SCOTT M. PURLEE

JOHNNY LIKED TO HAVE A "TASTE"

ROBERT GUINAN

Blues musicians were a Sunday morning fixture in the Maxwell Street open-air market for decades. Johnny Young was one of these. A heavyset man, he and his group anchored down a performance space that was set under three flights of unpainted tenement back steps.

Johnny liked to drink: — "to have a taste." But some long ago city administration, trying to get people out of taverns and into churches had made it illegal to sell alcohol before Noon on Sundays in Chicago. John knew of a "before-hours" place that existed to remedy the situation. It was a speakeasy: two rooms in the basement of a 19th century 3-flat near the market. The smaller room was apparently the living area of the solid, no-nonsense proprietress. In the larger room were four tables with tube chairs, and three refrigerators festooned with locks and chains. And there was a dog: a large, agitated boxer. A chain, fastened somewhere in the living area, allowed it to just reach the doorway between the two rooms. It could not be ignored. At one of the tables was a lone woman of late middle age dressed in Sunday best that included a modestly flamboyant hat. She was having a quiet drink either before or after church.

Johnny was self-effacing. His wife used to chide him for not promoting himself and his music as his old performing partner Muddy Waters had done. After he died in 1974, I learned through the writings of British music historian Mike Rowe that Johnny had been a pioneer. In 1947, after the war-time recording ban had been lifted, the owner of the Maxwell Street Radio Record Company approached four of the market performers to wax two 78 RPMs. Johnny's side was "Money Talking Woman." These were the first recorded examples of the new postwar music that would soon become known as the Chicago Blues.

He was one for the books.

PHOTOGRAPH TOM PALAZZOLO

DOUBLE DEUCE

JOHN PLATT

Across a frozen alley

 one of these lucky days

chasing two fluttering twenties

with all the world's forgotten

treasures waiting

in a burning junk store one

road-blocked block away.

AT MAXWELL STREET: A FILM BY TOM PALAZZOLO AND FRIENDS

NOTE ON THE DVD BY BILL STAMETS

In a belated match between the quintessential Chicago documentary filmmaker and an archetypal Chicago social phenomenon, Tom Palazzolo made the film *At Maxwell Street*. That street and this artist shared a kindred hustle and humor.

Since the Sunday morning market at Maxwell and Halsted Streets was the first place that so many students went with a camera, it might be expected to be the last place a seasoned documentary filmmaker would go back to. In fact, Palazzolo did shoot some of his first documentary footage there of Casey Jones (a.k.a. Chicken Charley). It is only fitting that he returned with beginning film students. It was the city's best site for free enterprise, flee market, black market, blues bands on the corner, watch bands up to the elbow, fresh fruit and greasy sausage, hawking, and gawking. There was a steady parade of picture-takers passing stands, booths, stalls, and heaps of merchandise. They wore Nikons as jewelry. They sought icons of poverty.

As a graduate student at the School of the Art Institute of Chicago in the early 1960s, Palazzolo began making experimental films like *Theorist's Room*, which was featured at the Chicago Filmmakers

Ten Year Anniversary program in 1985. As time went on, his interest shifted toward documenting the indigenous absurdities of Chicagoland. As portraits, these films always held a warm regard for individuals in the vernacular, typically marginals. In 1967, he made *The Story: How I Became the Tattooed Woman of Riverview*. In short, her boyfriend felt funny kissing her as the Bearded Lady, so she took the Sword-Swallower's advice and got tattooed. All manner of social occasions and minor rituals have drawn his attention for over forty years. In detail and in editing he has shown off a surreal, juvenile wit. Departing from this idiosyncratic style, Palazzolo embarked on a feature-length, semi-autobiographical narrative film with only a few sets and a fragment of a script. The resulting film, *Calagari's Cure* (1982), and its sequel *Added Lessons* (1988), used many art students and performance artists as actors.

At Maxwell Street similarly depended on a large degree of student involvement. Since his documentary filmmaking course was scheduled for Sundays, Palazzolo would take the class to Maxwell Street for practice handling 16mm film equipment. The film combined this footage shot by a score of students, some shot by Rodney Quirconi, and old footage found at Maxwell Street by Deborah Meehan, an experimental filmmaker. When Palazzolo taught at the University of Wisconsin in the summer of 1982, the film *Milwaukee Today* resulted from similar field trips with his filmmaking students.

Palazzolo especially liked the group effort that went into making *At Maxwell Street*. With his small group wending its way through the Sunday morning crowd, his filmmaking process was entirely public. Interaction between teacher and students, and between class and the street made for an appealing atmosphere of open participation. At random a bystander decided to become an impromptu interviewer; a vendor employing modest English skills was asked what ethnic groups are the hardest to deal with. The bystander concludes that as long as customers show a lot of respect, that's what counts. Pricing a leather coat, the sound-woman told the saleswoman where to get a good deal on plane tickets to Florida. The coat costs less afterwards.

The stories and stores, faces and façades, raps and deals are documented in a style suggesting equal footing between Palazzolo and Maxwell Street. He pretended no moral authority, historical erudition, sociological insight, or voyeur's hubris. From some of the dumb questions he and his students asked, there is not even much of a semblance of insider-status. The filmmakers surely were sympathetic. Their subjects were hardly undone by the crew's attention.

The folks at Howard's Style Shop nearly got away with turning the film into their own home movie in one segment. Back on the street, when the camera caught a pair of prostitutes, they declined a chance to appear, excusing themselves with mocking laughs. A freelance retailer of Seiko watches, though, conducted his business from a wheelchair and abided the camera for the sake of not risking a lost sale.

At Maxwell Street demonstrated a remarkable mode of filmmaking. To let a handful of beginning students aim camera and microphone is taking chances. Instead of a primer of errors, Palazzolo achieved an honest essay. On camera and on soundtrack he occasionally attempted to instruct his student crew. He kept in a segment where no one knew that the camera was still running. A quality of awkwardness and improvisation came about which fits the action indigenous to the street. Though his pedagogy may appear scattershot, Palazzolo's film was stamped with his characteristic humanism, relish of oddballs, and instinct for mysterious detail. His editing harmonized a phenomenological grab-bag of disparate footage without homogenizing its true roughness. The music Paul Gartski created for the film is entrancing, and is an essential ingredient. The discipline Palazzolo exercised over his many sources is subtle and winning.

Intercutting anonymous footage of peddlers cooking, musicians playing, and police arresting, Palazzolo underscores a theme of an exhibit curated by Larry Viskochil at the Chicago Historical Society. Documentary photographs by Nathan Lerner in the 1930s, and by James Newberry in the 1960s and 1970s demonstrated an amazing sameness about the street's scenes. Chicago documentarians and Maxwell Street were made for each other. And if you had gotten there early enough, you could of bought some real cheap film stock there. Honest.

(Based on a manuscript originally submitted to Chicago Reader)

AT MAXWELL STREET 1982 FILM CREDITS

Tom Palazzolo and Film Students from the School of the Art Institute of Chicago

Directed, photographed and edited by Tom Palazzolo
Vintage 1960s footage: Rodney Quiriconi
Vintage found footage: Courtesy Deborah Meehan
Music: Paul Gartski
Opticals: Tatsu Aoki

Additional Camera & Sound: (Participating Students)

Betty Alperstein	Henry Jackson
Marian Rotman	Maureen Clearfield
Laurie Muldoon	Kimmer Olesak
Yan Phoa	Duane Johnson
Jan Sugar	Joyce Suris
Jamirta Trotx	DeWitt Williams
Dan Perkins	Florence Gray
Roberta Rodriquez	Eric Leonardson
Karl Sandburg	Mike Byrne
Peter Keenan	Toba Zaritsky
Kapra Fleming	Joe Mouton
Ron Richardson	Peggy Wright
Donald Delaney	Jack Dugan
Jill Friedman	

Special thanks, to Kimmer Olesak for the "Shell Game"

Dedicated to the memory of filmmaker Allen Ross who helped with the film and lived in the Maxwell Street area.